Mastering

TRADING INDICATOR

by

Lalit Mohanty

PREFACE

VWAP is a powerful trading indicator that provides valuable insights into market dynamics, liquidity, and price trends. By understanding how to interpret and leverage VWAP analysis, traders can make informed trading decisions, optimize trade execution, and achieve consistent profitability across diverse market conditions.

In this book, we delve into the intricacies of VWAP trading, covering a wide range of topics including the basics of VWAP calculation, its significance in market analysis, and practical strategies for integrating VWAP into your trading approach. From trend analysis to risk management, from intraday strategies to options trading, each chapter offers valuable insights and actionable techniques to help you elevate your VWAP trading skills to the next level.

Table of Contents

CHAPTER 1

INTRODUCTION TO VWAP TRADING

Understanding VWAP (Volume Weighted Average Price)

VWAP, or Volume Weighted Average Price, is a powerful trading indicator used by traders and investors to gauge the average price of a financial instrument over a specific period, weighted by its trading volume. It is a dynamic metric that reflects both price and volume, providing insights into the true average price at which a particular asset has traded throughout the day.

Components of VWAP:

1. Price Component:

- VWAP calculates the average price at which a security has traded during a given period, incorporating all executed trades regardless of their size.

2. Volume Component:

- Unlike simple moving averages, VWAP considers trading volume, assigning higher weight to periods with greater trading activity. This feature makes VWAP particularly useful for assessing the significance of price movements in relation to trading volume.

Calculation Formula:

The VWAP formula is calculated by summing up the price times volume for every transaction and dividing it by the total trading volume within the specified time period. Mathematically, it can be represented as:

$$VWAP = \Sigma(\text{price x volume})/\Sigma(\text{volume})$$

where:

- *Price* represents the price of each transaction,

- *Volume* represents the corresponding volume of each transaction,

- The summation is performed over all transactions within the defined time frame.

Timeframes:

VWAP can be calculated over various timeframes, such as intraday (e.g., 1-minute, 5-minute, or 15-minute intervals) or longer periods (e.g., daily or weekly). Shorter timeframes provide insights into intraday trading dynamics, while longer timeframes offer a broader perspective on price trends.

Importance of VWAP in Trading

VWAP holds significant importance in trading for several reasons:

1. Execution Quality Assessment:

- Traders often benchmark their trade executions against VWAP to assess the quality of their trades. A trade executed below VWAP indicates a favorable execution, while a trade above VWAP suggests a less favorable execution.

2. Market Participation Analysis:

- VWAP helps traders understand market participation dynamics by highlighting periods of intense trading activity and price discovery. Sudden deviations of the current price from VWAP may indicate significant market interest or intervention.

3. Intraday Trading Strategies:

- VWAP serves as a key component in various intraday trading strategies, including trend following, mean reversion, and breakout strategies. Traders utilize VWAP to identify potential entry and exit points based on price-vol...

4. Risk Management:

- Incorporating VWAP into risk management strategies allows traders to adjust their position sizes based on the prevailing market conditions. Understanding how price movements relate to VWAP helps traders mitigate risks and protect their capital.

Historical Development of VWAP

The concept of VWAP traces back to the early days of algorithmic trading and institutional trading desks. Originally developed as a tool for institutional traders to evaluate their execution performance, VWAP gained popularity among retail traders due to its effectiveness in analyzing market dynamics.

Key Milestones in the Development of VWAP:

1. Institutional Adoption:

- VWAP was initially used by institutional traders to assess the impact of large orders on the market and to execute trades efficiently without causing significant price movements.

2. Algorithmic Trading:

- With the rise of algorithmic trading, VWAP became a standard benchmark for measuring algorithm performance and optimizing trade execution strategies.

3. Retail Trader Accessibility:

- The proliferation of electronic trading platforms and charting software made VWAP accessible to retail traders, enabling them to incorporate institutional-grade analytics into their trading strategies.

4. Integration with Technical Analysis:

- Over time, VWAP became an integral part of technical analysis, offering valuable insights into market trends, support and resistance levels, and trade entry/exit points.

Conclusion

VWAP is a versatile trading indicator that provides valuable insights into market dynamics, execution quality, and intraday trading opportunities. Understanding the calculation, interpretation, and historical development of VWAP is essential for traders seeking to harness its full potential in their trading endeavors. In the subsequent chapters, we will delve deeper into various VWAP trading strategies, ranging from basic to advanced techniques, to equip you with the knowledge and skills to master VWAP trading effectively.

CHAPTER 2

BASICS OF MARKET STRUCTURE

Order Types and Execution

Understanding the different order types and their execution mechanisms is crucial for comprehending how trades are facilitated in financial markets. Various order types allow traders to specify their trading instructions and preferences, influencing the dynamics of price discovery and liquidity provision.

Common Order Types:

1. Market Orders:

- Market orders are executed at the prevailing market price, ensuring immediate trade execution. They prioritize speed over price, making them suitable for traders seeking instant execution.

2. Limit Orders:

- Limit orders specify a price at which traders are willing to buy or sell an asset. They are executed only when the market price reaches the specified limit price, allowing traders to control the price at which their orders are filled.

3. Stop Orders:

- Stop orders become market orders once a specified price level (the stop price) is reached. They are commonly used for entering or exiting positions at predetermined price levels, particularly in volatile markets.

4. Stop-Limit Orders:

- Stop-limit orders combine elements of stop orders and limit orders. They trigger a limit order once the stop price is reached, ensuring that trades are executed within a specified price range.

5. Market-on-Close (MOC) Orders:

- MOC orders are executed at the closing price of the trading day, allowing traders to participate in the closing auction process. They are commonly used by institutional investors to manage their end-of-day positions.

Understanding the characteristics and implications of different order types is essential for devising effective trading strategies and optimizing trade execution.

Market Participants and their Impact on VWAP

Market participants play a pivotal role in shaping market dynamics and influencing VWAP movements. Different types of market participants, including retail traders, institutional investors, market makers, and high-frequency traders, exhibit distinct trading behaviors and objectives, which collectively contribute to the formation of VWAP.

1. Retail Traders:

- Retail traders comprise individual investors who trade for personal accounts. Their trading decisions are influenced by various factors, including market sentiment, technical analysis, and fundamental analysis. While retail traders may not individually impact VWAP significantly, their collective trading activity can contribute to intraday price volatility.

2. Institutional Investors:

- Institutional investors, such as mutual funds, hedge funds, and pension funds, execute large orders on behalf of their clients or stakeholders. These orders often have a significant impact on VWAP, particularly during the opening and closing auction periods. Institutional trading desks employ sophisticated VWAP algorithms to execute large orders efficiently while minimizing market impact.

3. Market Makers:

- Market makers facilitate liquidity provision by continuously quoting bid and ask prices for financial assets. They play a crucial role in maintaining orderly markets and narrowing bid-ask spreads. Market makers' trading activity can influence VWAP movements, especially in less liquid markets or during periods of heightened volatility.

4. High-Frequency Traders (HFTs):

- High-frequency traders employ algorithmic trading strategies to execute a large number of orders at extremely high speeds. HFTs capitalize on market inefficiencies and exploit short-term price movements for profit. Their rapid trading activity can contribute to intraday price fluctuations and impact VWAP calculations.

Understanding the behavior and objectives of different market participants is essential for interpreting VWAP movements and anticipating potential market trends.

Market Microstructure and VWAP

Market microstructure refers to the mechanics and dynamics of how orders are processed, matched, and executed within financial markets. It encompasses various elements, including order books, trading venues, order routing mechanisms, and market regulations, all of which influence VWAP calculations and trading outcomes.

Key Components of Market Microstructure:

1. Order Books:

- Order books display a real-time list of buy and sell orders for a particular asset, along with their respective prices and quantities. Order book dynamics, such as order imbalances and depth of liquidity, can impact VWAP movements by affecting supply and demand dynamics.

2. Trading Venues:

- Trading venues, such as stock exchanges, electronic communication networks (ECNs), and alternative trading systems (ATSs), serve as platforms for executing trades. Different trading venues may have distinct order matching algorithms and fee structures, which can influence VWAP calculations and execution costs.

3. Order Routing:

- Order routing refers to the process of directing trade orders to various trading venues or liquidity pools for execution. Smart order routing algorithms aim to optimize trade execution by considering factors such as price, liquidity, and market impact. Effective order routing strategies can help minimize slippage and improve VWAP performance.

4. Market Regulations:

- Market regulations, enforced by regulatory authorities, govern trading activities and ensure fair and orderly markets. Regulations related to trade reporting, market manipulation, and insider trading play a crucial role in maintaining market integrity and transparency, thereby indirectly impacting VWAP calculations.

Understanding the intricacies of market microstructure is essential for VWAP traders to navigate the complexities of financial markets and make informed trading decisions.

Conclusion

A solid grasp of market structure fundamentals lays the groundwork for effective VWAP trading strategies. By understanding the mechanics of order types, the behavior of market participants, and the dynamics of market microstructure, traders can gain valuable insights into VWAP movements and enhance their trading performance. In the subsequent chapters, we will explore advanced VWAP trading strategies and techniques to further leverage the power of VWAP in the dynamic world of financial markets.

CHAPTER 3

SETTING UP YOUR TRADING PLATFORM

Choosing the Right Trading Platform

Selecting the appropriate trading platform is a critical decision for traders, as it directly impacts their ability to analyze markets, execute trades efficiently, and integrate essential trading tools such as VWAP. When choosing a trading platform, traders should consider several factors:

1. User Interface and Experience:

- A user-friendly interface with intuitive navigation enhances the trading experience and reduces the learning curve for new users. Look for platforms that offer customizable layouts and streamlined workflows to accommodate individual preferences.

2. Market Access and Instrument Coverage:

- Ensure that the trading platform provides access to the markets and financial instruments you intend to trade, including stocks, options, futures, forex, and cryptocurrencies. Comprehensive instrument coverage enables diversification and flexibility in trading strategies.

3. Order Execution Speed and Reliability:

- Fast and reliable order execution is essential for capturing market opportunities and minimizing slippage. Evaluate the platform's execution speed, uptime reliability, and order routing capabilities to ensure seamless trade execution across various market conditions.

4. Charting and Technical Analysis Tools:

- Robust charting features and technical analysis tools are indispensable for conducting thorough market analysis and identifying trading opportunities. Look for platforms that offer a wide range of indicators, drawing tools, and customization options to support your trading strategy.

5. Integration with Third-Party Software:

- Consider whether the trading platform allows integration with third-party software and APIs (Application Programming Interfaces) for advanced analysis, algorithmic trading, and automated strategies. Compatibility with popular trading software and programming languages enhances the platform's versatility and functionality.

6. Cost and Fees:

- Evaluate the pricing structure, including commissions, fees, and subscription plans, to determine the cost-effectiveness of the trading platform. Compare pricing models across different platforms and consider the value proposition in relation to the features and services offered.

Configuring VWAP on Different Platforms

Once you've selected a trading platform that meets your requirements, it's essential to configure VWAP to incorporate it into your trading workflow effectively. While specific steps may vary depending on the platform, the general process typically involves:

1. Accessing Charting Tools:

- Navigate to the charting or analysis section of the trading platform where you can customize technical indicators and overlays.

2. Adding VWAP Indicator:

- Locate the VWAP indicator among the available technical indicators or overlays provided by the platform. In most cases, you can find VWAP under volume or trend indicators categories.

3. Adjusting Parameters:

- Customize VWAP parameters such as time frame (e.g., intraday, daily, weekly), calculation method (standard or anchored), and display settings (line color, style, thickness) to align with your trading preferences.

4. Saving Settings:

- Save the configured VWAP settings as a template or default layout to streamline future analysis and ensure consistency across different trading sessions.

5. Testing and Validation:

- Test the VWAP indicator on historical data or paper trading to validate its performance and familiarize yourself with its behavior under various market conditions.

Customizing VWAP Parameters

Customizing VWAP parameters allows traders to adapt the indicator to their specific trading objectives and market preferences. Some common parameters that traders may customize include:

1. Time Frame:

- Adjust the time frame over which VWAP is calculated, such as intraday (e.g., 1-minute, 5-minute, 15-minute intervals) or longer periods (e.g., daily, weekly).

2. Anchored VWAP:

- Choose between standard VWAP, which resets at the beginning of each trading day, or anchored VWAP, which starts calculations from a specified reference point, such as a significant event or time period.

3. VWAP Bands:

- Add standard deviation bands or percentage deviation bands around VWAP to visualize volatility and potential support/resistance levels.

4. Volume Weighting:

- Modify the weighting scheme for VWAP calculations, such as equal weighting or volume weighting based on trade size or transaction volume.

5. Display Settings:

- Customize the visual appearance of the VWAP line, including color, style, thickness, and transparency, to enhance visibility and readability on the chart.

By customizing VWAP parameters according to their trading style and market analysis requirements, traders can leverage the indicator more effectively as part of their trading strategy.

Conclusion

Setting up your trading platform and configuring VWAP are crucial steps in establishing a solid foundation for effective trading. By choosing the right trading platform that aligns with your trading goals and preferences, configuring VWAP to suit your analysis needs, and customizing its parameters to enhance its effectiveness, you can optimize your trading experience and maximize your chances of success in the dynamic world of financial markets. In the subsequent chapters, we will delve deeper into specific VWAP trading strategies and techniques to further enhance your trading proficiency.

CHAPTER 4

CALCULATING VWAP

Mathematical Formulas

VWAP, or Volume Weighted Average Price, is a key indicator used in financial markets to assess the average price at which a security has traded over a specified period, weighted by its trading volume. The mathematical formula for calculating VWAP is relatively straightforward:

VWAP = Σ(price x volume)/Σ(volume)

where:

- *Price* represents the price of each transaction,

- *Volume* represents the corresponding volume of each transaction,

- The summation is performed over all transactions within the defined time frame.

The VWAP calculation aggregates the product of each trade's price and volume and divides it by the total trading volume within the specified time period. This process results in a single average price that reflects both price and volume considerations.

Real-Time VWAP Calculation

Real-time VWAP calculation involves continuously updating the VWAP value as new trades occur throughout the trading session. Traders often use real-time VWAP to monitor intraday price trends, assess trade execution quality, and identify potential entry and exit points.

The real-time VWAP calculation process typically involves the following steps:

1. Initialize Variables:

- Set initial variables such as cumulative price, cumulative volume, and VWAP.

2. Receive New Trade Data:

- Receive incoming trade data, including trade price and volume, from the market feed.

3. Update Cumulative Values:

- Update cumulative price and volume by adding the price and volume of the new trade to the existing totals.

4. Calculate VWAP:

- Recalculate VWAP using the updated cumulative price and volume values based on the VWAP formula.

5. Repeat:

- Continuously repeat steps 2-4 for each new trade received, ensuring that VWAP is updated in real-time.

Real-time VWAP calculation provides traders with up-to-date information on intraday price dynamics and helps them make informed trading decisions in rapidly changing market conditions.

Intraday vs. Daily VWAP

While VWAP can be calculated over various timeframes, two common variants are intraday VWAP and daily VWAP. Each serves a distinct purpose and provides unique insights into market behavior.

1. Intraday VWAP:

- Intraday VWAP calculates the average price of a security over a single trading session or intraday period, such as 1-minute, 5-minute, or 15-minute intervals. Intraday VWAP is particularly useful for assessing intraday price trends, identifying trading opportunities, and evaluating trade execution quality throughout the trading day.

2. Daily VWAP:

- Daily VWAP calculates the average price of a security over the entire trading day, from the market open to close. Daily VWAP provides a broader perspective on price trends and market sentiment for the entire trading session. It is commonly used by institutional traders and investors to benchmark their performance against the market's average price and assess the impact of large orders on VWAP.

While both intraday and daily VWAP offer valuable insights into market dynamics, traders may choose to use one or both variants depending on their trading objectives and time horizon.

Conclusion

Understanding how to calculate VWAP, both in real-time and over different timeframes, is essential for traders seeking to leverage this powerful indicator in their trading strategies. By mastering the mathematical formulas behind VWAP, monitoring real-time VWAP updates, and distinguishing between intraday and daily VWAP calculations, traders can gain valuable insights into price trends, volume dynamics, and trade execution performance. In the subsequent chapters, we will explore various VWAP trading strategies and applications to further enhance your trading proficiency.

CHAPTER 5

VWAP AS A BENCHMARK

VWAP, or Volume Weighted Average Price, serves as a benchmark for traders and investors to evaluate trade execution quality, assess market trends, and gauge the relative value of securities. In this chapter, we will explore how VWAP is used as a benchmark, its effectiveness in assessing trade performance, and its limitations in certain trading scenarios.

Comparing Trades Against VWAP

One of the primary uses of VWAP is to compare individual trade executions against the VWAP value to assess whether trades were executed at favorable or unfavorable prices. Traders typically analyze the following scenarios:

1. Trade Below VWAP:

- A trade executed below VWAP indicates that the transaction price was lower than the average price paid by market participants throughout the trading session. This suggests a favorable execution, as the trader bought at a price lower than the average market price.

2. Trade Above VWAP:

- Conversely, a trade executed above VWAP implies that the transaction price exceeded the average market price. This signifies a less favorable execution, as the trader paid a premium compared to the average market price.

Comparing trades against VWAP allows traders to assess the efficiency of their trade execution and identify areas for improvement in their trading strategies.

Assessing Trade Performance Using VWAP

VWAP also serves as a performance benchmark for evaluating the effectiveness of trading strategies and individual trades. Traders use VWAP as a reference point to assess the following aspects of trade performance:

1. Trade Efficiency:

- Traders aim to achieve trade executions close to or better than VWAP to demonstrate efficient order routing and execution strategies. Consistently trading below VWAP indicates skillful execution and effective price negotiation.

2. Market Impact:

- Deviations from VWAP may indicate the impact of large trades on market prices. Trades executed significantly above or below VWAP may suggest market impact and liquidity constraints, particularly for large orders.

3. Trade Analysis:

- Analyzing trades relative to VWAP provides insights into market dynamics, trader behavior, and trading patterns. Traders can identify trends, correlations, and anomalies by comparing trade performance metrics against VWAP over different timeframes.

By evaluating trade performance using VWAP as a benchmark, traders can gain valuable insights into their execution quality, market timing, and overall trading effectiveness.

Limitations of VWAP as a Benchmark

While VWAP is a widely used benchmark in trading, it has certain limitations that traders should be aware of:

1. Sensitivity to Volume Distribution:

- VWAP may be sensitive to volume distribution, particularly in thinly traded markets or during periods of low liquidity. Extreme volume spikes or imbalances can skew VWAP calculations and distort its accuracy as a benchmark.

2. Intraday Variability:

- Intraday VWAP values fluctuate continuously as new trades occur throughout the trading session. Traders should consider the intraday variability of VWAP when using it as a benchmark for trade analysis and decision-making.

3. Market Regime Changes:

- VWAP may be less effective as a benchmark during periods of market regime changes, such as high volatility, news events, or structural shifts. Traders should supplement VWAP analysis with additional indicators and market insights to adapt to changing market conditions.

While VWAP provides valuable insights into trade execution and market trends, traders should use it in conjunction with other metrics and indicators to make well-informed trading decisions.

Conclusion

VWAP serves as a versatile benchmark for evaluating trade performance, assessing market trends, and gauging the relative value of securities. By comparing trades against VWAP, assessing trade performance using VWAP as a reference point, and recognizing its limitations in certain trading scenarios, traders can leverage VWAP effectively as part of their trading arsenal. In the subsequent chapters, we will explore advanced VWAP trading strategies and techniques to further enhance your trading proficiency.

CHAPTER 6

USING VWAP IN TREND ANALYSIS

VWAP, or Volume Weighted Average Price, can be a valuable tool for identifying trends, distinguishing between trend reversals and continuations, and integrating with other technical indicators to enhance trend analysis. In this chapter, we will explore how VWAP is utilized in trend analysis and its integration with other technical tools.

Identifying Trends with VWAP

VWAP can help traders identify trends by providing a reference point for assessing the direction and strength of price movements relative to average market prices. Traders typically analyze the following aspects to identify trends using VWAP:

1. Trend Direction:

- Consistent deviations of the current price from VWAP may indicate the presence of a trend. Prices trading above VWAP suggest an uptrend, while prices trading below VWAP suggest a downtrend.

2. Trend Magnitude:

- The distance between the current price and VWAP can provide insights into the magnitude of the trend. Larger deviations from VWAP indicate stronger trends, while smaller deviations may signal weaker or range-bound market conditions.

3. Trend Duration:

- Monitoring VWAP over different timeframes allows traders to assess the duration and persistence of trends. Prolonged deviations of prices from VWAP across multiple timeframes suggest sustained trends, while short-lived deviations may indicate temporary fluctuations.

By analyzing price movements relative to VWAP, traders can identify trends and adapt their trading strategies accordingly.

Trend Reversals vs. Continuations

VWAP can also assist traders in distinguishing between trend reversals and continuations, providing insights into potential turning points in the market. Traders typically look for the following signals to identify trend reversals and continuations using VWAP:

1. Trend Reversals:

- Reversal patterns occur when prices reverse direction after a prolonged trend. Traders may look for price crossing VWAP from one side to the other, accompanied by significant volume spikes, as potential signals of trend reversals.

2. Trend Continuations:

- Continuation patterns occur when prices continue to move in the direction of the prevailing trend. Traders may observe prices consistently trading above or below VWAP, accompanied by steady volume, as indications of trend continuations.

By monitoring price movements relative to VWAP and volume dynamics, traders can anticipate trend reversals and continuations and adjust their trading strategies accordingly.

Integrating VWAP with Other Technical Indicators

VWAP can be integrated with other technical indicators to enhance trend analysis and improve trading decisions. Traders often combine VWAP with the following technical tools for comprehensive trend analysis:

1. Moving Averages:

- Combining VWAP with traditional moving averages (e.g., simple moving average, exponential moving average) allows traders to validate trends and identify potential trend crossovers. Crosses between VWAP and moving averages can signal trend changes and trading opportunities.

2. Bollinger Bands:

- Overlaying Bollinger Bands, which represent volatility bands around a moving average, with VWAP can help traders identify overbought and oversold conditions within trending markets. Price rejections at Bollinger Bands in conjunction with VWAP can indicate potential trend reversals or continuations.

3. Relative Strength Index (RSI):

- Integrating RSI, a momentum oscillator, with VWAP allows traders to assess the strength of trends and potential trend exhaustion points. Divergences between RSI and VWAP may signal trend reversals or continuations, providing valuable confirmation signals.

By combining VWAP with other technical indicators, traders can gain deeper insights into market trends, confirm trend signals, and make more informed trading decisions.

Conclusion

VWAP is a versatile tool for trend analysis, helping traders identify trends, distinguish between trend reversals and continuations, and integrate with other technical indicators for comprehensive analysis. By monitoring price movements relative to VWAP, assessing trend dynamics, and leveraging VWAP in conjunction with other technical tools, traders can enhance their trend analysis capabilities and improve their trading strategies. In the subsequent chapters, we will explore advanced VWAP trading strategies and techniques to further refine your trend analysis skills.

CHAPTER 7

VWAP AND VOLUME ANALYSIS

Volume analysis plays a crucial role in understanding market dynamics and interpreting price movements. When combined with VWAP (Volume Weighted Average Price), traders gain valuable insights into volume patterns, price trends, and potential trading opportunities. In this chapter, we will explore how VWAP and volume analysis are integrated to analyze volume profiles, identify volume clusters and breakouts, and correlate volume with price movements.

Analyzing Volume Profiles

Volume profiles provide a visual representation of trading volume at different price levels within a specified time period. By analyzing volume profiles in conjunction with VWAP, traders can identify key support and resistance levels, assess market sentiment, and anticipate potential price reversals or continuations.

1. Value Area:

- The value area represents the price range where the majority of trading volume occurs. Traders often focus on price levels within the value area as potential areas of price equilibrium and trading opportunities.

2. Volume Gaps:

- Volume gaps, or areas with significant gaps in trading volume, may indicate areas of low liquidity or price inefficiencies. Traders pay attention to volume gaps as potential support or resistance zones where price may exhibit rapid movements.

Volume Clusters and Breakouts

Volume clusters occur when trading volume accumulates around specific price levels, signaling potential areas of interest for market participants. Traders use volume clusters in conjunction with VWAP to identify breakout opportunities and gauge the strength of price movements.

1. High Volume Nodes:

- High volume nodes represent price levels with significant trading volume. Breakouts above or below high volume nodes accompanied by increasing volume may signal the emergence of strong trends or directional movements.

2. Low Volume Areas:

- Low volume areas, conversely, denote price levels with relatively low trading volume. Traders monitor low volume areas for potential breakouts or reversals, as a sudden influx of volume may indicate a shift in market sentiment or participation.

Correlating Volume with Price Movements

Volume analysis can provide valuable confirmation signals for price movements and trend reversals. By correlating volume with VWAP and price action, traders can validate trend signals, assess market breadth, and anticipate potential changes in market direction.

1. Volume Confirmation:

- Increasing volume accompanying price movements in the direction of the trend validates the strength of the trend and enhances the likelihood of trend continuation. Conversely, declining volume amid price movements may signal weakening momentum or potential trend reversals.

2. Volume Divergence:

- Divergences between volume and price movements can provide early warning signals for trend reversals or exhaustion. Traders watch for discrepancies between volume and price action, such as declining volume amid rising prices or increasing volume with limited price movements, as potential signs of trend exhaustion.

Conclusion

VWAP and volume analysis are powerful tools for traders seeking to understand market dynamics, identify trading opportunities, and make informed trading decisions. By analyzing volume profiles, identifying volume clusters and breakouts, and correlating volume with price movements, traders can gain deeper insights into market sentiment, trend dynamics, and potential price reversals or continuations. In the subsequent chapters, we will explore advanced VWAP trading strategies and techniques to further leverage the power of VWAP and volume analysis in trading.

CHAPTER 8

BASIC VWAP TRADING STRATEGIES

VWAP (Volume Weighted Average Price) is a versatile trading indicator that can be applied in various trading strategies. In this chapter, we will explore three basic VWAP trading strategies: mean reversion strategies, momentum strategies, and opening range breakouts.

Mean Reversion Strategies

Mean reversion strategies aim to capitalize on price reversals towards the mean, exploiting temporary deviations from the average market price. Traders utilizing mean reversion strategies with VWAP typically look for opportunities to enter trades when prices deviate significantly from VWAP, expecting prices to revert back to the mean.

Strategy Components:

1. **Identifying Overextended Moves:** Traders monitor price movements relative to VWAP, looking for instances where prices move excessively away from VWAP, signaling potential overextensions.

2. **Entry Points:** Once a significant deviation from VWAP is identified, traders look for entry points to establish positions in the opposite direction, anticipating price reversals towards VWAP.

3. **Exit Strategy:** Traders may exit positions once prices revert back towards VWAP or when the deviation from VWAP diminishes, locking in profits from the mean reversion trade.

Momentum Strategies

Momentum strategies aim to capitalize on the continuation of existing price trends, leveraging the momentum of price movements. While VWAP is primarily a mean-reverting indicator, it can also be used in conjunction with other momentum indicators to identify and confirm trending markets.

Strategy Components:

1. **Confirming Trends:** Traders assess the alignment of price trends with VWAP to confirm the strength and direction of momentum. Prices consistently trading above VWAP may signal an uptrend, while prices below VWAP may indicate a downtrend.

2. **Entry Points:** Traders look for entry points in the direction of the prevailing trend, such as pullbacks towards VWAP in uptrends or bounces off VWAP in downtrends, to enter trades in alignment with momentum.

3. **Exit Strategy:** Traders may exit positions once momentum starts to weaken or when prices deviate significantly from VWAP, signaling potential trend reversals or exhaustion.

Opening Range Breakouts

Opening range breakout strategies capitalize on price movements following the opening of the trading session, exploiting breakouts above or below the initial trading range. VWAP can serve as a reference point for assessing opening range breakouts and identifying potential breakout opportunities.

Strategy Components:

1. **Establishing Opening Range:** Traders define the opening range by identifying the highest and lowest prices traded within the initial trading period, typically the first hour of trading.

2. **Breakout Confirmation:** Traders wait for prices to break out above the high of the opening range in an uptrend or below the low of the opening range in a downtrend, confirming potential breakout signals.

3. **Entry Points:** Traders enter positions once breakout signals are confirmed, anticipating continued price momentum in the direction of the breakout.

4. **Exit Strategy:** Traders may exit positions based on predefined profit targets or when prices fail to sustain the breakout momentum, potentially signaling false breakouts or trend reversals.

Conclusion

Basic VWAP trading strategies encompass a range of approaches, including mean reversion, momentum, and breakout strategies, each offering distinct opportunities for traders to capitalize on market dynamics. By understanding the components and principles of these strategies, traders can adapt their trading approach to different market conditions and enhance their trading proficiency. In the subsequent chapters, we will delve deeper into advanced VWAP trading strategies and techniques to further refine your trading skills.

CHAPTER 9

INTRADAY VWAP STRATEGIES

Intraday VWAP strategies are tailored to capitalize on price movements and volume dynamics within a single trading session. Traders utilize different approaches at different times of the trading day to align with market conditions and maximize trading opportunities. In this chapter, we will explore opening, midday, and closing intraday VWAP strategies.

Opening Strategies

1. VWAP Reversion to the Mean:

- **Objective:** Capitalize on early price deviations from VWAP that tend to revert back towards the mean.

- **Execution:** Enter trades in the opposite direction of the initial price gap from VWAP, anticipating price reversals towards VWAP.

- **Timing:** Execute trades shortly after the market open to capture early morning volatility and liquidity.

2. Opening Range Breakouts:

- **Objective:** Exploit breakout opportunities following the establishment of the opening price range.

- **Execution:** Wait for prices to break out above or below the high or low of the opening range, confirming potential breakout signals.

- **Timing:** Monitor price movements during the first hour of trading to identify breakout opportunities.

Midday Strategies

1. Trend Continuation:

- **Objective:** Ride intraday trends that persist beyond the initial opening range.

- **Execution:** Enter trades in the direction of the prevailing trend, aligning with VWAP and other trend indicators.

- **Timing:** Look for entry opportunities during periods of sustained momentum and volume participation.

2. Pullback Entries:

- **Objective:** Capitalize on temporary pullbacks within established intraday trends.

- **Execution:** Enter trades on pullbacks towards VWAP or key support/resistance levels within trending markets.

- **Timing:** Identify pullback opportunities during periods of price retracement amid ongoing trends.

Closing Strategies

1. VWAP Pinning:

- **Objective:** Exploit end-of-day price action as prices gravitate towards VWAP during the closing auction.

- **Execution:** Enter trades aligned with VWAP positioning during the final minutes of trading, anticipating price convergence towards VWAP.

- **Timing:** Execute trades strategically to capture price movements during the closing auction period.

2. Volume Surges:

- **Objective:** Trade on increased volume activity during the final trading hour, anticipating significant price movements.

- **Execution:** Monitor volume surges and price momentum during the closing hour, entering trades in the direction of volume spikes.

- **Timing:** Focus on trading opportunities arising from heightened volume participation towards the end of the trading day.

Conclusion

Intraday VWAP strategies offer traders a range of approaches to navigate the dynamic price and volume dynamics within a single trading session. By leveraging opening, midday, and closing strategies, traders can adapt their trading approach to different stages of the trading day and capitalize on intraday trading opportunities. In the subsequent chapters, we will explore advanced VWAP trading strategies and techniques to further refine your intraday trading skills.

CHAPTER 10

SWING TRADING WITH VWAP

Swing trading is a trading style that aims to capture short- to medium-term price movements within an established trend. Traders employing swing trading strategies seek to capitalize on swings or "swings" in asset prices, typically holding positions for several days to weeks. In this chapter, we will explore swing trading basics, utilizing VWAP (Volume Weighted Average Price) to identify swing points, and managing risk in swing trades.

Swing Trading Basics

Swing trading involves entering and exiting positions based on the anticipated direction of price swings within a broader trend. Traders employing swing trading strategies typically follow these key principles:

1. Trend Identification:

- Traders identify established trends using technical analysis tools and indicators to determine the direction of price movements. Common trend-following indicators include moving averages, trendlines, and price patterns.

2. Entry and Exit Signals:

- Traders enter swing trades at opportune moments, such as pullbacks or breakouts, aligning with the prevailing trend. Entry signals may be generated by technical indicators or price action patterns. Traders exit positions when price reaches predetermined profit targets or when the trend shows signs of reversal.

3. Risk Management:

- Managing risk is paramount in swing trading to preserve capital and mitigate losses. Traders employ stop-loss orders to limit potential losses and adhere to predefined risk-reward ratios for each trade.

Using VWAP to Identify Swing Points

VWAP can be integrated into swing trading strategies to identify potential swing points and validate trade setups. Traders utilize VWAP in conjunction with other technical indicators to confirm trend direction and assess market sentiment. Here's how VWAP can be used in swing trading:

1. Swing Highs and Lows:

- VWAP can act as a reference point for identifying swing highs and lows within a trend. Traders look for price reversals or bounces near VWAP, signaling potential swing points.

2. Confirmation Signals:

- Traders seek confirmation from VWAP to validate swing trading setups. Price bouncing off VWAP in the direction of the trend may serve as a confirmation signal for entering swing trades.

3. Volume Analysis:

- Volume dynamics around VWAP can provide insights into the strength of price swings and potential trend reversals. Increased volume activity near VWAP may indicate significant market participation and validate swing trading opportunities.

Managing Risk in Swing Trades

Risk management is critical in swing trading to protect capital and ensure long-term profitability. Traders employ various risk management techniques to control risk exposure and optimize trade outcomes:

1. Stop-loss Orders:

- Traders set stop-loss orders at predefined levels to limit potential losses in swing trades. Stop-loss orders are placed below swing lows (for long trades) or above swing highs (for short trades) to minimize risk.

2. Position Sizing:

- Traders determine position size based on their risk tolerance and the distance to the stop-loss level. Position sizing ensures that each trade's risk is proportionate to the trader's overall account size and risk appetite.

3. Risk-Reward Ratio:

- Traders assess risk-reward ratios for each trade to ensure that potential profits outweigh potential losses. A favorable risk-reward ratio, typically 2:1 or higher, enhances the probability of long-term profitability in swing trading.

Conclusion

Swing trading with VWAP offers traders a systematic approach to capturing short- to medium-term price swings within established trends. By adhering to swing trading basics, utilizing VWAP to identify swing points, and implementing effective risk management techniques, traders can enhance their swing trading performance and achieve consistent trading results. In the subsequent chapters, we will delve deeper into advanced VWAP trading strategies and techniques to further refine your swing trading skills.

CHAPTER 11

OPTIONS TRADING WITH VWAP

Options trading offers unique opportunities for traders to leverage volatility and market dynamics. By incorporating VWAP (Volume Weighted Average Price) into options strategies, traders can enhance their decision-making process, optimize trade execution, and manage risk more effectively. In this chapter, we will explore how VWAP can be integrated into options trading strategies, its relationship with implied volatility, and how to utilize VWAP to time options trades.

Incorporating VWAP into Options Strategies

VWAP can be incorporated into various options strategies to enhance trade analysis and execution. Traders utilize VWAP in conjunction with options pricing models, technical indicators, and market insights to inform their options trading decisions. Here are some ways VWAP can be integrated into options strategies:

1. Options Spreads:

- Traders analyze VWAP to identify optimal entry and exit points for options spreads, such as vertical spreads, iron condors, and butterfly spreads. VWAP can help traders gauge the fair value of options and assess the liquidity of options contracts.

2. Volatility Strategies:

- VWAP can be used to gauge market volatility and assess the attractiveness of volatility-based options strategies, such as straddles, strangles, and volatility skews. Traders monitor VWAP in conjunction with implied volatility levels to identify opportunities for volatility trades.

3. Delta-Neutral Strategies:

- Traders employing delta-neutral options strategies, such as delta hedging and gamma scalping, utilize VWAP to manage their options positions and hedge against directional risk. VWAP can help traders adjust their options exposure based on market dynamics and price movements.

Implied Volatility and VWAP

Implied volatility, a key component of options pricing, reflects market expectations of future volatility. VWAP can provide valuable insights into implied volatility levels and help traders assess options pricing relative to historical volatility and trading volume. Here's how VWAP relates to implied volatility in options trading:

1. Volatility Clusters:

- Traders analyze VWAP and implied volatility clusters to identify periods of heightened volatility and potential trading opportunities. VWAP can help traders gauge the magnitude and duration of volatility clusters, aiding in options strategy selection and risk management.

2. Options Pricing:

- VWAP serves as a reference point for assessing options pricing relative to implied volatility levels. Traders compare VWAP-derived fair value with options premiums to determine whether options are overvalued or undervalued, informing their options trading decisions.

3. Volatility Skews:

- Traders monitor VWAP and implied volatility skews to identify skew patterns and potential deviations from the norm. VWAP can help traders assess the impact of volatility skews on options pricing and adjust their options strategies accordingly.

Using VWAP to Time Options Trades

Timing is crucial in options trading, and VWAP can be a valuable tool for timing options trades and optimizing trade execution. Traders utilize VWAP to identify favorable entry and exit points for options trades based on market dynamics and price movements. Here's how VWAP can be used to time options trades effectively:

1. VWAP Crosses:

- Traders monitor VWAP crosses, where price crosses above or below VWAP, as potential entry or exit signals for options trades. VWAP crosses can indicate shifts in market sentiment and price trends, informing options trading decisions.

2. Volume Confirmation:

- Traders seek confirmation from volume dynamics around VWAP to validate options trading setups. Increased volume activity near VWAP may confirm options trade signals and enhance trade conviction.

3. VWAP Bands:

- Traders utilize VWAP bands, such as standard deviation bands or percentage deviation bands around VWAP, to identify potential support and resistance levels for options trades. VWAP bands can help traders set price targets and manage risk in options positions.

Conclusion

Options trading with VWAP offers traders a systematic approach to analyzing options pricing, assessing implied volatility, and timing options trades effectively. By incorporating VWAP into options strategies, understanding its relationship with implied volatility, and utilizing VWAP to time options trades, traders can enhance their options trading performance and achieve consistent results. In the subsequent chapters, we will delve deeper into advanced VWAP trading strategies and techniques to further refine your options trading skills.

CHAPTER 12

ADVANCED VWAP TECHNIQUES

In the fast-paced world of financial markets, traders are constantly seeking ways to gain an edge and improve trading performance. Advanced VWAP techniques leverage sophisticated statistical analysis, machine learning algorithms, and adaptive strategies to enhance trade execution, optimize risk management, and adapt to evolving market conditions. In this chapter, we will explore advanced VWAP techniques, including advanced statistical analysis, machine learning applications, and adaptive VWAP strategies.

Advanced Statistical Analysis

Advanced statistical analysis techniques allow traders to extract deeper insights from VWAP data and identify hidden patterns or anomalies in market behavior. Traders utilize statistical methods such as regression analysis, time series analysis, and volatility modeling to analyze VWAP data and make informed trading decisions. Here's how advanced statistical analysis can enhance VWAP trading:

1. Regression Analysis:

- Traders employ regression analysis to model the relationship between VWAP and other market variables, such as volume, volatility, and price. Regression models help traders identify factors influencing VWAP dynamics and anticipate future price movements.

2. Time Series Analysis:

- Time series analysis techniques, including autoregressive integrated moving average (ARIMA) models and exponential smoothing methods, allow traders to forecast VWAP trends and detect underlying patterns in VWAP data over time. Time series analysis aids in predicting future VWAP levels and optimizing trade timing.

3. Volatility Modeling:

- Traders use volatility modeling techniques, such as GARCH (Generalized Autoregressive Conditional Heteroskedasticity) models and stochastic volatility models, to estimate and forecast market volatility. Volatility models help traders adjust VWAP-based strategies to changing market volatility conditions and manage risk more effectively.

Machine Learning and VWAP

Machine learning algorithms offer powerful tools for analyzing complex market data and extracting predictive insights from VWAP time series. Traders leverage machine learning techniques, including supervised learning, unsupervised learning, and reinforcement learning, to develop predictive models, optimize trading strategies, and automate trade execution. Here's how machine learning can be applied to VWAP trading:

1. Predictive Modeling:

- Traders train machine learning models to predict future VWAP levels based on historical market data and relevant features, such as price, volume, and market sentiment indicators. Predictive models help traders anticipate VWAP trends and make timely trading decisions.

2. Pattern Recognition:

- Machine learning algorithms excel at recognizing complex patterns and anomalies in VWAP data that may not be apparent to human traders. Traders use pattern recognition techniques, such as clustering analysis and anomaly detection, to identify hidden trading opportunities and potential market inefficiencies.

3. Algorithmic Trading:

- Traders deploy machine learning-based algorithms for algorithmic trading strategies that leverage VWAP data for automated trade execution. Algorithmic trading algorithms continuously analyze VWAP dynamics, adjust trading parameters in real-time, and execute trades at optimal price levels, enhancing trading efficiency and liquidity provision.

Adaptive VWAP Strategies

Adaptive VWAP strategies dynamically adjust trade execution parameters based on evolving market conditions, ensuring optimal trade execution and risk management. Traders utilize adaptive VWAP strategies to adapt to changing market volatility, liquidity, and price dynamics in real-time. Here's how adaptive VWAP strategies work:

1. Market Adaptation:

- Adaptive VWAP algorithms monitor market conditions, such as volume spikes, price volatility, and order book dynamics, and adjust trade execution parameters, such as participation rates and aggression levels, to optimize trade execution performance.

2. Dynamic Benchmarking:

- Adaptive VWAP strategies dynamically benchmark trade execution performance against changing market conditions and adjust trading strategies accordingly. Traders continuously evaluate VWAP performance relative to alternative benchmarks, such as arrival price or implementation shortfall, and adapt trading strategies to minimize market impact and slippage.

3. Machine Learning Integration:

- Adaptive VWAP strategies integrate machine learning algorithms to learn from past trading experiences, adapt to evolving market dynamics, and optimize trade execution parameters in real-time. Machine learning algorithms analyze historical trade data, market variables, and trading outcomes to refine adaptive VWAP strategies and improve trading performance over time.

Conclusion

Advanced VWAP techniques empower traders with sophisticated tools and methodologies to gain a competitive edge in financial markets. By leveraging advanced statistical analysis, machine learning algorithms, and adaptive VWAP strategies, traders can enhance trade execution precision, optimize risk management, and adapt to changing market conditions with agility and precision. In the subsequent chapters, we will explore case studies and practical applications of advanced VWAP techniques in real-world trading scenarios.

CHAPTER 13

VWAP AND MARKET SENTIMENT

Market sentiment, the collective mood or attitude of market participants towards a particular asset or market, plays a significant role in influencing price movements and trading dynamics. VWAP (Volume Weighted Average Price) provides valuable insights into market sentiment by reflecting the average price at which trades are executed weighted by volume. In this chapter, we will explore the relationship between VWAP and market sentiment, the impact of news and events on VWAP, and strategies for trading with or against market sentiment.

Sentiment Analysis and VWAP

1. Trend Identification:

- VWAP can act as a sentiment indicator, reflecting the prevailing sentiment of market participants. Prices consistently trading above VWAP may indicate bullish sentiment, while prices below VWAP may suggest bearish sentiment.

2. Volume Dynamics:

- Changes in trading volume around VWAP can provide clues about shifts in market sentiment. Increasing volume accompanying price movements may confirm prevailing sentiment, while divergences between volume and price may signal sentiment shifts.

3. VWAP Deviations:

- Significant deviations of prices from VWAP may indicate extremes in market sentiment. Prices deviating significantly above VWAP may signal overbought conditions and bullish sentiment exhaustion, while prices below VWAP may indicate oversold conditions and bearish sentiment exhaustion.

News and Event Impact on VWAP

1. Event-Driven Volatility:

- News announcements, economic releases, and geopolitical events can trigger volatility spikes and impact VWAP dynamics. VWAP may deviate significantly from its normal trajectory in response to unexpected news events, reflecting shifts in market sentiment and trading activity.

2. Volume Spikes:

- News-driven events often result in increased trading volume and volatility, leading to notable volume spikes around VWAP. Volume spikes accompanied by price movements away from VWAP may signal shifts in market sentiment and provide trading opportunities.

3. Reversion to VWAP:

- Following news-driven price movements, prices often revert back towards VWAP as market participants reassess the impact of news events on market fundamentals. Traders monitor VWAP reversion patterns to gauge the sustainability of sentiment-driven price moves.

Trading Against or with Market Sentiment

1. Contrarian Strategies:

- Contrarian traders often trade against prevailing market sentiment, entering positions when sentiment extremes are reached and anticipating mean reversion towards VWAP. Contrarian strategies aim to profit from sentiment reversals and market overreactions.

2. Trend-Following Strategies:

- Trend-following traders, on the other hand, align their trading strategies with prevailing market sentiment, entering positions in the direction of the trend and riding momentum away from VWAP. Trend-following strategies aim to capture profits from sustained price movements driven by sentiment dynamics.

3. Sentiment Confirmation:

- Some traders combine sentiment analysis with VWAP to confirm trading signals and improve trade conviction. They may wait for sentiment confirmation from VWAP dynamics before entering trades, ensuring alignment with prevailing market sentiment.

Conclusion

VWAP provides valuable insights into market sentiment by reflecting the average price at which trades are executed weighted by volume. By analyzing VWAP dynamics, volume patterns, and deviations from

VWAP, traders can assess market sentiment, anticipate sentiment-driven price movements, and develop effective trading strategies. Whether trading against or with market sentiment, understanding the relationship between VWAP and market sentiment is essential for making informed trading decisions in dynamic market environments. In the subsequent chapters, we will explore case studies and practical applications of VWAP and market sentiment analysis in real-world trading scenarios.

CHAPTER 14

VWAP AND ALGORITHMIC TRADING

Algorithmic trading has revolutionized financial markets by automating trade execution and optimizing trading strategies using advanced mathematical models and computer algorithms. VWAP (Volume Weighted Average Price) is a key tool in algorithmic trading, offering valuable insights into market dynamics and optimizing trade execution efficiency. In this chapter, we will explore algorithmic trading, the incorporation of VWAP into trading algorithms, and the role of VWAP in high-frequency trading (HFT) strategies.

Algorithmic Trading Overview

1. Automation:

- Algorithmic trading involves the use of computer algorithms to execute trades automatically based on predefined trading rules and parameters. Algorithms analyze market data, identify trading opportunities, and execute trades with minimal human intervention.

2. Efficiency:

- Algorithmic trading algorithms are designed to optimize trade execution efficiency by minimizing transaction costs, reducing market impact, and maximizing trade profitability. Algorithms execute trades at optimal price levels and times to achieve the best possible trade outcomes.

3. Diversification:

- Algorithmic trading allows traders to diversify their trading strategies across multiple markets, assets, and timeframes. Algorithms can simultaneously execute trades across different exchanges and instruments, spreading risk and maximizing trading opportunities.

Incorporating VWAP into Algorithms

1. Trade Execution:

- Algorithms incorporate VWAP into trade execution algorithms to optimize trade execution efficiency. VWAP-based algorithms aim to execute trades at or near the VWAP price to minimize market impact and achieve better trade outcomes.

2. Participation Rates:

- Algorithms adjust participation rates dynamically based on VWAP dynamics to optimize trade execution. Higher participation rates may be employed when prices are trading near VWAP, while lower participation rates may be used during periods of high volatility or deviation from VWAP.

3. Benchmarking:

- Algorithms benchmark trade execution performance against VWAP to evaluate trade effectiveness and minimize tracking error. Algorithms compare realized trade prices with VWAP levels to assess trade quality and adjust trading strategies accordingly.

High-Frequency Trading and VWAP

1. Speed and Efficiency:

- High-frequency trading (HFT) strategies leverage VWAP to execute trades with lightning-fast speed and efficiency. HFT algorithms analyze VWAP dynamics in real-time and execute trades within milliseconds to exploit fleeting market opportunities.

2. Liquidity Provision:

- HFT algorithms act as liquidity providers by continuously quoting bid and ask prices around the VWAP, facilitating price discovery and improving market liquidity. HFT algorithms adjust quote sizes and prices dynamically based on VWAP movements to maintain optimal liquidity provision.

3. Arbitrage Opportunities:

- HFT algorithms identify arbitrage opportunities by exploiting discrepancies between VWAP and other market indicators or exchange prices. HFT algorithms execute trades rapidly to capitalize on temporary mispricings and generate profits from market inefficiencies.

Conclusion

VWAP plays a crucial role in algorithmic trading by optimizing trade execution efficiency, minimizing market impact, and enhancing trade profitability. By incorporating VWAP into trading algorithms, traders can achieve better trade outcomes, reduce transaction costs, and improve overall trading performance. In high-frequency trading

(HFT) strategies, VWAP serves as a key benchmark for trade execution and provides valuable insights into market liquidity and pricing dynamics. Understanding the relationship between VWAP and algorithmic trading is essential for traders looking to leverage VWAP effectively in automated trading strategies. In the subsequent chapters, we will delve deeper into case studies and practical applications of VWAP in algorithmic trading scenarios.

CHAPTER 15

DEVELOPING A VWAP TRADING PLAN

.

A well-defined trading plan is essential for successful trading with VWAP (Volume Weighted Average Price). It provides a structured framework for executing trades, managing risk, and achieving trading objectives. In this chapter, we will explore the key components of developing a VWAP trading plan, including creating a comprehensive trading plan, implementing risk management strategies specific to VWAP trading, and conducting backtesting to validate VWAP trading strategies.

Creating a Comprehensive Trading Plan

1. Define Trading Objectives:

- Identify your trading goals, such as profit targets, risk tolerance, and timeframes. Determine whether you're trading VWAP for short-term intraday trades, swing trading, or longer-term investments.

2. Strategy Selection:

- Choose the VWAP trading strategies that align with your trading goals and risk profile. Consider whether you'll be using VWAP for mean reversion, trend following, or breakout trading strategies.

3. Trade Execution:

- Outline your trade execution plan, including entry and exit criteria, trade sizes, and position management rules. Define how you'll use VWAP to determine trade entry and exit points.

4. Market Analysis:

- Specify the market analysis tools and indicators you'll use alongside VWAP, such as volume analysis, trend indicators, and price action patterns. Determine how you'll integrate these tools into your trading plan.

5. Review and Adjustment:

- Regularly review and adjust your trading plan based on changing market conditions, performance metrics, and evolving trading objectives. A trading plan is a dynamic document that should adapt to your experience and market environment.

Risk Management with VWAP

1. Position Sizing:

- Determine the size of each trade relative to your account size and risk tolerance. Consider using a percentage of capital approach or fixed monetary risk per trade to manage position sizes effectively.

2. Stop-loss Orders:

- Implement stop-loss orders to limit potential losses on each trade. Place stop-loss levels based on VWAP deviations, support/resistance levels, or volatility measures to minimize downside risk.

3. Volatility Adjustments:

- Adjust position sizes and stop-loss levels based on market volatility. Increase position sizes in low-volatility environments and reduce risk exposure during periods of high volatility to maintain consistent risk management.

4. Portfolio Diversification:

- Diversify your trading portfolio to spread risk across different asset classes, markets, and trading strategies. Avoid overexposure to a single asset or market segment to minimize portfolio risk.

Backtesting VWAP Strategies

1. Historical Data:

- Gather historical market data, including price, volume, and VWAP levels, for the period you intend to backtest. Use reputable data sources and ensure data quality and accuracy.

2. Strategy Implementation:

- Implement your VWAP trading strategies using historical data, simulating trade executions based on predefined entry and exit criteria. Use backtesting software or trading platforms with backtesting capabilities for accurate simulation.

3. Performance Analysis:

- Analyze the performance of your VWAP trading strategies using backtesting results. Evaluate key performance metrics such as profitability, win rate, maximum drawdown, and risk-adjusted returns to assess strategy effectiveness.

4. Optimization:

- Optimize your VWAP trading strategies based on backtesting results, refining entry and exit criteria, adjusting risk management parameters, and identifying areas for improvement. Iteratively backtest and refine your strategies until you achieve satisfactory results.

Conclusion

Developing a comprehensive VWAP trading plan is essential for achieving consistent trading success. By outlining clear trading objectives, implementing effective risk management strategies, and conducting thorough backtesting, traders can build robust VWAP trading strategies and enhance their trading performance. A well-defined trading plan provides a roadmap for navigating volatile markets, managing risk, and achieving long-term trading success with VWAP. In the subsequent chapters, we will explore case studies and practical applications of VWAP trading plans in real-world trading scenarios.

CHAPTER 16

PSYCHOLOGICAL ASPECTS OF VWAP TRADING

Trading with VWAP (Volume Weighted Average Price) involves not only technical analysis and strategy implementation but also the management of psychological factors that can significantly impact trading performance. In this chapter, we will explore the psychological aspects of VWAP trading, including the influence of emotions, the importance of patience and discipline, and strategies for overcoming common psychological mistakes.

Emotions and Trading

1. Fear and Greed:

- Fear and greed are common emotions that can influence trading decisions. Fear of missing out (FOMO) may lead traders to chase price movements away from VWAP, while fear of losses may prevent traders from taking valid trading signals.

Greed may cause traders to hold onto winning trades for too long or increase position sizes beyond their risk tolerance.

2. Overconfidence:

- Overconfidence can lead traders to overestimate their abilities and take excessive risks. Traders may become overconfident in their VWAP trading strategies, leading to reckless decision-making and poor risk management.

3. Impatience:

- Impatience can result in premature trade exits or entries based on impulsive decisions rather than following the trading plan. Traders may struggle to wait for valid VWAP signals to develop, leading to missed opportunities or losses.

Patience and Discipline with VWAP

1. Stick to the Trading Plan:

- Maintain discipline by adhering to your VWAP trading plan, including entry and exit criteria, risk management rules, and trade execution guidelines. Avoid deviating from the plan based on emotions or impulsive decisions.

2. Exercise Patience:

- Practice patience by waiting for high-probability trade setups aligned with VWAP signals. Avoid rushing into trades or exiting prematurely before the trade thesis has played out. Patience allows traders to capitalize on favorable market conditions and avoid impulsive decisions.

3. Control Emotions:

- Develop emotional resilience by managing fear, greed, and other emotions that can impact trading decisions. Utilize techniques such as mindfulness, deep breathing, or journaling to maintain emotional balance during trading.

Overcoming Common Mistakes

1. Avoid Overtrading:

- Overtrading can deplete trading capital and increase transaction costs. Focus on quality over quantity by waiting for high-probability trade setups based on VWAP signals and avoiding excessive trading activity.

2. Cut Losses Quickly:

- Learn to accept losses and cut losing trades quickly to minimize losses and preserve capital. Set predefined stop-loss levels based on VWAP deviations or technical support/resistance levels and adhere to them rigorously.

3. Review and Learn:

- Continuously review your trading performance, identify areas for improvement, and learn from mistakes. Keep a trading journal to track trades, analyze outcomes, and identify patterns in behavior or decision-making that may need adjustment.

Conclusion

The psychological aspects of VWAP trading play a significant role in shaping trading outcomes. By recognizing the influence of emotions, practicing patience and discipline, and actively working to overcome common psychological mistakes, traders can improve their VWAP trading performance and achieve greater consistency in their results. Developing emotional resilience and psychological discipline is essential for navigating the challenges of VWAP trading and maintaining a successful trading mindset. In the subsequent chapters, we will explore case studies and practical strategies for managing psychological factors in VWAP trading.

CHAPTER 17

VWAP IN DIFFERENT MARKETS

VWAP (Volume Weighted Average Price) is a versatile trading indicator that can be applied across various financial markets, including equities, forex, commodities, and cryptocurrencies. In this chapter, we will explore how VWAP is utilized in different markets, highlighting its significance, applications, and variations across diverse asset classes.

Applying VWAP to Equities

1. Market Execution:

- In equity markets, VWAP is commonly used by institutional traders and algorithmic trading systems for benchmarking trade execution performance. Traders aim to execute orders close to the VWAP to minimize market impact and achieve favorable trade outcomes.

2. Intraday Analysis:

- Day traders and short-term investors utilize intraday VWAP to identify trading opportunities and gauge market sentiment. VWAP deviations from the intraday price can signal shifts in market dynamics and potential trade setups.

3. Volume Analysis:

- VWAP provides insights into volume dynamics and liquidity levels in equity markets. Traders analyze VWAP alongside volume profiles and order book data to assess market participation and potential price reversals.

VWAP in Forex and Commodities

1. Liquidity Benchmark:

- In the forex and commodities markets, VWAP serves as a benchmark for measuring trade execution efficiency and assessing market liquidity. Traders aim to execute trades close to the VWAP to minimize slippage and transaction costs.

2. Trend Confirmation:

- Forex and commodities traders use VWAP to confirm trend directions and identify potential trend reversals. VWAP deviations from the prevailing trend may signal changes in market sentiment and provide trading opportunities.

3. Timeframe Adaptation:

- Traders adjust VWAP parameters based on the trading timeframe and market conditions. Shorter-term traders may use intraday VWAP for day trading, while longer-term investors may employ daily or weekly VWAP for trend analysis.

VWAP in Cryptocurrency Markets

1. Execution Efficiency:

- In cryptocurrency markets, VWAP is utilized by traders and exchanges to optimize trade execution efficiency and minimize price slippage. Traders aim to execute orders close to the VWAP to achieve better trade outcomes.

2. Market Analysis:

- Cryptocurrency traders use VWAP to analyze market dynamics, assess trading volume, and identify liquidity levels. VWAP deviations in cryptocurrency prices may indicate changes in market sentiment and trading activity.

3. Algorithmic Trading:

- Algorithmic trading strategies in cryptocurrency markets leverage VWAP for automated trade execution and liquidity provision. High-frequency trading (HFT) algorithms use VWAP to capture fleeting market opportunities and maintain optimal liquidity provision.

Conclusion

VWAP is a versatile trading indicator that finds application across a wide range of financial markets, including equities, forex, commodities, and cryptocurrencies. Whether used for benchmarking trade execution, analyzing market dynamics, or confirming trend directions, VWAP provides valuable insights into market sentiment, liquidity, and price trends across different asset classes. Traders can adapt VWAP-based strategies to suit various market conditions and trading objectives, making it a valuable tool in the trader's toolkit across diverse trading environments. In the subsequent chapters, we will explore case studies and practical applications of VWAP in different market scenarios.

CHAPTER 18

REAL-WORLD CASE STUDIES

Real-world case studies provide valuable insights into the practical application of VWAP (Volume Weighted Average Price) trading strategies in dynamic market environments. By examining successful trades, learning from failed trades, and analyzing notable market events, traders can gain valuable lessons and refine their VWAP trading approach. In this chapter, we will explore real-world case studies to illustrate the effectiveness, challenges, and lessons learned from VWAP trading.

Analyzing Successful VWAP Trades

Case Study 1: Intraday Trend Continuation

- **Trade Setup:** A trader identifies an intraday trend continuation setup where price remains consistently above VWAP, indicating bullish sentiment.

- **Execution:** The trader enters a long position as price pulls back to VWAP support, aligning with the prevailing trend.

- **Outcome:** The trade results in a profitable outcome as price continues its upward trajectory, validating the bullish bias and VWAP support.

Case Study 2: Mean Reversion Bounce

- **Trade Setup:** A trader identifies a mean reversion setup where price deviates significantly below VWAP, indicating oversold conditions.

- **Execution:** The trader enters a long position as price bounces off VWAP support, anticipating a reversion to the mean.

- **Outcome:** The trade results in a profitable outcome as price retraces back towards VWAP, confirming the mean reversion thesis and generating profits for the trader.

Learning from Failed Trades

Case Study 3: False Breakout Reversal

- **Trade Setup:** A trader anticipates a breakout above VWAP resistance, entering a long position as price breaks out.

- **Execution:** However, the breakout fails to sustain, and price quickly reverses below VWAP, triggering the trader's stop-loss.

- **Outcome:** The trade results in a loss as the breakout proves to be a false signal, highlighting the importance of waiting for confirmation and managing risk.

Case Study 4: Choppy Market Whipsaw

- **Trade Setup:** A trader attempts to trade a choppy market environment, entering positions based on short-term VWAP deviations.

- **Execution:** However, the choppy price action results in multiple false signals and whipsaws, leading to consecutive losing trades.

- **Outcome:** The trader experiences losses due to the challenging market conditions, emphasizing the need to adapt trading strategies to volatile market environments.

Lessons from Notable Market Events

Case Study 5: Flash Crash of 2010

- **Event:** During the flash crash of 2010, market indices experienced a rapid and severe decline followed by a swift recovery within minutes.

- **Lesson:** VWAP proved to be an unreliable benchmark during extreme market events, as it failed to capture the extreme price movements accurately. Traders learned the importance of risk management and liquidity provision during volatile market conditions.

Case Study 6: Brexit Referendum

- **Event:** During the Brexit referendum in 2016, markets experienced heightened volatility and significant price gaps across various asset classes.

- **Lesson:** VWAP analysis provided valuable insights into market sentiment and price dynamics during the Brexit event. Traders learned the importance of adapting trading strategies to fast-changing market conditions and managing risk effectively.

Conclusion

Real-world case studies offer valuable learning opportunities for VWAP traders, highlighting successful trade setups, pitfalls to avoid, and lessons learned from notable market events. By analyzing successful trades, learning from failed trades, and dissecting significant market events, traders can refine their VWAP trading strategies, improve decision-making, and navigate dynamic market environments with confidence. Case studies provide practical insights into the application of VWAP in real-world trading scenarios, allowing traders to enhance their trading skills and achieve greater consistency in their trading results. In the subsequent chapters, we will explore additional case studies and practical applications of VWAP trading strategies in diverse market conditions.

CHAPTER 19

REVIEW OF TRADING PSYCHOLOGY

Trading psychology plays a crucial role in the success of VWAP (Volume Weighted Average Price) traders. Mastering emotional discipline, developing a winning mindset, and effectively managing trading stress are essential aspects of maintaining consistency and profitability in VWAP trading. In this chapter, we will review key concepts in trading psychology and explore practical strategies for enhancing psychological resilience and performance in VWAP trading.

Mastering Emotional Discipline

Understanding Emotions:

- Emotions such as fear, greed, and impatience can influence trading decisions. Recognizing and acknowledging these emotions is the first step toward mastering emotional discipline.

Emotional Regulation:

- Develop techniques to regulate emotions during trading, such as deep breathing exercises, mindfulness meditation, or taking breaks during stressful periods. Cultivating emotional awareness and self-control is essential for making rational trading decisions.

Stick to the Plan:

- Adhere to your VWAP trading plan rigorously, even in the face of emotional impulses or market fluctuations. Trust in your strategy and follow predefined rules for entry, exit, and risk management.

Developing a Winning Mindset

Positive Self-Talk:

- Foster a positive mindset by replacing self-doubt and negativity with affirmations and constructive self-talk. Cultivate confidence in your abilities as a trader and focus on continuous improvement.

Visualization:

- Visualize success and visualize yourself executing trades with confidence and precision. Mental rehearsal can help reinforce positive trading behaviors and prepare you for various market scenarios.

Learn from Setbacks:

- Embrace failures and setbacks as learning opportunities rather than defeats. Analyze losing trades objectively, extract lessons from mistakes, and use them to refine your VWAP trading approach.

Dealing with Trading Stress

Stress Management Techniques:

- Incorporate stress management techniques into your trading routine, such as exercise, relaxation exercises, or hobbies outside of trading. Maintaining a healthy work-life balance is crucial for reducing trading-related stress.

Risk Management:

- Implement effective risk management strategies to mitigate trading stress and preserve capital. Setting appropriate stop-loss levels and position sizes can alleviate anxiety and uncertainty during trading.

Focus on Process:

- Shift your focus from outcome-oriented thinking to process-oriented thinking. Instead of fixating on individual trade results, concentrate on following your trading plan and executing trades according to predefined criteria.

Conclusion

Trading psychology is a critical aspect of VWAP trading, influencing decision-making, performance, and overall trading outcomes. By mastering emotional discipline, developing a winning mindset, and effectively managing trading stress, traders can enhance their psychological resilience and achieve greater consistency in VWAP trading. Cultivating self-awareness, confidence, and mental fortitude is essential for navigating the challenges of trading and maintaining a successful trading career. In the subsequent chapters, we will delve deeper into practical techniques and case studies to further enhance trading psychology in VWAP trading.

CHAPTER 20

EVALUATING MARKET CONDITIONS WITH VWAP

Evaluating market conditions is crucial for effective trading, and VWAP (Volume Weighted Average Price) serves as a valuable tool for analyzing market dynamics across different conditions. In this chapter, we will explore how VWAP can be used to evaluate market conditions by examining its relationship with volatility, market regimes, and strategies for adapting to changing market conditions.

Volatility and VWAP

1. Volatility Impact:

- Volatility measures the magnitude of price fluctuations in the market. High volatility environments often result in wider price ranges and increased trading activity, while low volatility environments may lead to tighter ranges and reduced trading volume.

2. VWAP Sensitivity:

- VWAP can be sensitive to changes in market volatility. In high volatility conditions, VWAP may exhibit greater fluctuations and deviations from the prevailing price, reflecting increased trading activity and price uncertainty.

3. Adjusting Trading Strategies:

- Traders may adjust their VWAP trading strategies based on market volatility. In high volatility environments, traders may reduce trade sizes or widen stop-loss levels to account for increased price variability, while in low volatility conditions, traders may increase trade sizes or tighten risk parameters.

Market Regimes and VWAP

1. Trending Markets:

- In trending markets, VWAP can serve as a trend confirmation tool, validating the direction of the prevailing trend. Prices consistently trading above VWAP may indicate bullish trends, while prices below VWAP may suggest bearish trends.

2. Range-bound Markets:

- In range-bound markets, VWAP acts as a reference point for identifying support and resistance levels. Prices oscillating around VWAP may signify a balanced market with no clear directional bias, offering opportunities for mean reversion or breakout strategies.

3. Transitioning Between Regimes:

- Market regimes can transition between trending and range-bound conditions over time. Traders monitor VWAP dynamics and volume patterns to anticipate regime shifts and adjust trading strategies accordingly.

Adapting to Changing Market Conditions

1. Real-time Monitoring:

- Continuously monitor VWAP dynamics and market conditions in real-time to adapt to changing environments. Use VWAP deviations, volume analysis, and price action signals to gauge market sentiment and adjust trading strategies accordingly.

2. Flexible Trading Strategies:

- Develop flexible VWAP trading strategies that can adapt to different market conditions. Incorporate multiple VWAP parameters, such as intraday VWAP, daily VWAP, and volume-weighted standard deviation bands, to accommodate varying volatility levels and regime shifts.

3. Risk Management:

- Implement robust risk management practices to mitigate the impact of changing market conditions on trading performance. Set predefined risk parameters, including stop-loss levels, position sizes, and maximum drawdown limits, to protect capital during volatile or uncertain market periods.

Conclusion

VWAP provides valuable insights into market conditions by reflecting the average price at which trades are executed weighted by volume. By evaluating market conditions with VWAP, traders can adapt their trading strategies to changing volatility levels, identify prevailing market regimes, and optimize trade execution efficiency. Understanding the relationship between VWAP and market conditions is essential for making informed trading decisions and achieving consistent trading results across diverse market environments. In the subsequent chapters, we will explore practical applications and case studies of VWAP trading strategies in various market conditions.

CHAPTER 21

INTEGRATING FUNDAMENTAL ANALYSIS WITH VWAP

Integrating fundamental analysis with VWAP (Volume Weighted Average Price) trading strategies can provide traders with a comprehensive approach to decision-making by incorporating both market sentiment and fundamental factors. In this chapter, we will explore how fundamental analysis, including economic indicators, earnings reports, and mergers and acquisitions (M&A), can be integrated with VWAP to enhance trading insights and decision-making.

Economic Indicators and VWAP

1. Market Reaction to Economic Data:

- Economic indicators, such as GDP growth, inflation rates, and employment data, can influence market sentiment and price movements. Traders monitor VWAP dynamics following the release of key economic data to gauge market reactions and sentiment shifts.

2. Volatility and VWAP:

- High-impact economic events often lead to increased market volatility, impacting VWAP dynamics. Traders analyze VWAP deviations and volume patterns around economic releases to assess the strength of market sentiment and potential trading opportunities.

3. Trend Confirmation:

- Economic indicators can confirm or contradict prevailing market trends reflected in VWAP dynamics. Positive economic data may validate bullish trends, while negative data may signal trend reversals or corrections.

Earnings Reports and VWAP

1. Earnings Season Impact:

- During earnings seasons, companies release financial results that can significantly impact stock prices and market sentiment. Traders analyze VWAP behavior before and after earnings reports to assess market expectations and reactions.

2. Price Gaps and VWAP:

- Earnings surprises or misses often result in price gaps and sharp price movements, impacting VWAP dynamics. Traders monitor VWAP deviations and volume patterns following earnings announcements to identify trading opportunities.

3. Volume Analysis:

- Volume analysis alongside VWAP can provide insights into market participation and liquidity levels during earnings-related price movements. High volume spikes around earnings events may indicate increased investor interest and trading activity.

Mergers and Acquisitions Impact on VWAP

1. Market Sentiment Shifts:

- Mergers, acquisitions, or corporate announcements can lead to significant shifts in market sentiment and price dynamics. Traders analyze VWAP behavior before and after M&A announcements to gauge market reactions and sentiment shifts.

2. Arbitrage Opportunities:

- M&A announcements may create arbitrage opportunities, leading to price dislocations and deviations from VWAP. Traders monitor VWAP dynamics and volume patterns to identify mispricings and capitalize on arbitrage opportunities.

3. Risk Management:

- M&A events can introduce uncertainty and volatility into the market, impacting risk management strategies. Traders adjust risk parameters, including stop-loss levels and position sizes, to mitigate the impact of M&A-related price movements on trading performance.

Conclusion

Integrating fundamental analysis with VWAP trading strategies enhances traders' ability to make informed decisions by incorporating both market sentiment and fundamental factors. By analyzing economic indicators, earnings reports, and M&A announcements alongside VWAP dynamics, traders can gain valuable insights into market dynamics, identify trading opportunities, and manage risk effectively. Understanding the relationship between fundamental factors and VWAP behavior is essential for developing robust trading strategies and achieving consistent trading results across various market conditions. In the subsequent chapters, we will explore practical applications and case studies of integrating fundamental analysis with VWAP trading strategies.

CHAPTER 22

BUILDING CUSTOM VWAP STRATEGIES

Custom VWAP (Volume Weighted Average Price) strategies offer traders the flexibility to tailor their trading approach to suit their unique trading styles, preferences, and objectives. Whether focusing on intraday scalping, swing trading, or long-term investing, customizing VWAP strategies allows traders to optimize trade execution efficiency and adapt to changing market conditions. In this chapter, we will explore the process of building custom VWAP strategies, including tailoring VWAP to your trading style, automating VWAP strategies, and continuously optimizing VWAP strategies for improved performance.

Tailoring VWAP to Your Trading Style

1. Scalping Strategies:

- For intraday scalping, traders may focus on short-term VWAP deviations and rapid trade execution. Adjust VWAP parameters, such as timeframes and smoothing factors, to capture short-term price movements and capitalize on intraday volatility.

2. Swing Trading Strategies:

- Swing traders may use VWAP to identify longer-term trends and trade setups. Utilize longer-term VWAP periods, such as daily or weekly VWAP, to confirm trend directions and establish swing trade entry and exit points based on VWAP support and resistance levels.

3. Position Trading Strategies:

- Position traders may employ VWAP as a benchmark for longer-term investment decisions. Monitor VWAP trends over extended periods, such as monthly or quarterly VWAP, to assess broader market sentiment and make informed position trading decisions.

Automating VWAP Strategies

1. Algorithmic Trading:

- Automate VWAP strategies using algorithmic trading systems or trading bots. Program VWAP-based algorithms to execute trades automatically based on predefined criteria, including VWAP deviations, volume thresholds, and price action signals.

2. Trade Automation Platforms:

- Utilize trade automation platforms or APIs to integrate VWAP strategies with trading platforms. Connect VWAP algorithms to market data feeds and execution platforms for seamless trade execution and real-time monitoring.

3. Backtesting and Optimization:

- Backtest and optimize automated VWAP strategies using historical market data. Fine-tune algorithm parameters, such as VWAP calculation methods and trade execution rules, to maximize profitability and minimize risk.

Continuous Optimization of VWAP Strategies

1. Performance Analysis:

- Continuously analyze the performance of VWAP strategies using real-time data and performance metrics. Monitor key indicators, such as win rate, average profit/loss, and maximum drawdown, to assess strategy effectiveness.

2. Adaptation to Market Conditions:

- Adapt VWAP strategies to changing market conditions and volatility levels. Adjust VWAP parameters dynamically based on current market dynamics, such as volatility bands, volume thresholds, and trend indicators.

3. Iterative Improvement:

- Iterate and improve VWAP strategies over time based on ongoing performance analysis and feedback. Experiment with new ideas, incorporate additional technical indicators, or refine risk management rules to enhance strategy performance and adaptability.

Conclusion

Building custom VWAP strategies allows traders to optimize trade execution efficiency, adapt to changing market conditions, and achieve their trading objectives. By tailoring VWAP to their trading style, automating VWAP strategies, and continuously optimizing VWAP strategies, traders can enhance their trading performance and achieve greater consistency in their results. Custom VWAP strategies provide traders with the flexibility and adaptability to navigate dynamic market environments and capitalize on trading opportunities effectively. In the subsequent chapters, we will explore practical applications and case studies of custom VWAP strategies in real-world trading scenarios.

CHAPTER 23

VWAP AND SEASONAL TRENDS

Seasonal trends play a significant role in shaping market dynamics, presenting unique opportunities for traders to capitalize on recurring patterns and market behavior. By incorporating VWAP (Volume Weighted Average Price) analysis into seasonal trading strategies, traders can identify, analyze, and exploit seasonal trends effectively. In this chapter, we will explore how VWAP can be used to identify seasonal patterns, trade seasonal trends, and adjust strategies to accommodate seasonal changes in market conditions.

Identifying Seasonal Patterns with VWAP

1. Historical Analysis:

- Conduct historical analysis using VWAP to identify seasonal patterns and recurring trends in market behavior. Analyze past data to identify seasonal trends associated with specific timeframes, such as months, quarters, or holidays.

2. Volume Analysis:

- Utilize volume analysis alongside VWAP to identify seasonal shifts in market participation and trading activity. High-volume periods may coincide with seasonal trends, indicating increased investor interest and potential trading opportunities.

3. Price Deviations:

- Monitor price deviations from VWAP during seasonal periods to identify anomalies or deviations from normal market behavior. Seasonal trends may manifest as consistent price movements above or below VWAP during specific timeframes.

Trading Seasonal Trends Using VWAP

1. Trend Confirmation:

- Use VWAP as a tool to confirm seasonal trends and validate market sentiment during seasonal periods. Prices consistently trading above or below VWAP may signal bullish or bearish seasonal trends, providing trading opportunities.

2. Entry and Exit Signals:

- Establish entry and exit signals based on VWAP dynamics during seasonal trends. Enter trades when prices deviate significantly from VWAP in the direction of the seasonal trend and exit positions as prices revert back towards VWAP.

3. Risk Management:

- Implement robust risk management strategies to mitigate the impact of seasonal volatility on trading performance. Set appropriate stop-loss levels, position sizes, and risk parameters based on seasonal patterns and market conditions.

Adjusting Strategies for Seasonal Changes

1. Dynamic Parameter Adjustment:

- Adjust VWAP parameters, such as calculation periods or smoothing factors, to accommodate seasonal changes in market volatility and trading activity. Shorten or lengthen VWAP periods to align with seasonal trends and optimize trade execution.

2. Adaptive Position Sizing:

- Adapt position sizing based on seasonal volatility levels and risk profiles. Increase position sizes during high-confidence seasonal trends and reduce exposure during periods of uncertainty or volatility.

3. Flexibility in Trading Approach:

- Maintain flexibility in trading approach to adapt to changing seasonal conditions and market dynamics. Utilize a combination of VWAP-based strategies, technical indicators, and fundamental analysis to capitalize on seasonal trends effectively.

Conclusion

VWAP analysis provides traders with a powerful tool for identifying, analyzing, and trading seasonal trends in financial markets. By incorporating VWAP into seasonal trading strategies, traders can gain valuable insights into market behavior, confirm seasonal trends, and optimize trade execution efficiency. Adjusting strategies for seasonal changes allows traders to adapt to evolving market conditions and capitalize on seasonal opportunities effectively. Seasonal trading using VWAP provides traders with a systematic approach to navigating seasonal trends and achieving consistent trading results across diverse market environments. In the subsequent chapters, we will explore practical applications and case studies of seasonal trading strategies using VWAP analysis.

CHAPTER 24

VWAP AND RISK MANAGEMENT

Risk management is a critical aspect of trading that aims to protect capital and minimize losses while maximizing profitability. Integrating VWAP (Volume Weighted Average Price) analysis into risk management strategies allows traders to make informed decisions regarding stop-loss and take-profit levels, position sizing, and risk adjustments based on market conditions. In this chapter, we will explore how VWAP can be used to enhance risk management techniques, including setting stop-loss and take-profit levels, position sizing, and adjusting risk based on market conditions.

Setting Stop-Loss and Take-Profit Levels with VWAP

1. VWAP Deviations:

- Use VWAP deviations as a guide for setting stop-loss and take-profit levels. Place stop-loss orders below VWAP for long positions and above VWAP for short positions to limit potential losses. Take-profit levels can be set at VWAP deviations in the direction of the trade.

2. Support and Resistance:

- Identify VWAP as dynamic support and resistance levels to determine stop-loss and take-profit levels. Prices consistently trading above VWAP may act as support for long positions, while prices below VWAP may serve as resistance for short positions.

3. Volume Confirmation:

- Confirm stop-loss and take-profit levels with volume analysis alongside VWAP. High-volume areas around VWAP deviations may reinforce the validity of stop-loss and take-profit levels, indicating significant market interest and potential price reversals.

Position Sizing with VWAP

1. Volatility Adjustments:

- Adjust position sizes based on VWAP deviations and market volatility. Increase position sizes during low-volatility periods when prices are trading close to VWAP and decrease exposure during high-volatility periods to mitigate risk.

2. ATR Bands:

- Utilize Average True Range (ATR) bands alongside VWAP to determine position sizes. Set position sizes based on ATR multiples to accommodate fluctuations in market volatility and align risk exposure with current market conditions.

3. VWAP Bands:

- Define position sizes based on VWAP deviation bands to manage risk effectively. Increase position sizes within VWAP bands and reduce exposure outside of VWAP bands to adapt to changing market dynamics and minimize losses.

Adjusting Risk Based on Market Conditions

1. Market Volatility:

- Adjust risk parameters, including stop-loss levels and position sizes, based on current market volatility levels. Tighten stop-loss levels and reduce position sizes during high-volatility periods to limit potential losses.

2. Trend Strength:

- Assess trend strength using VWAP analysis to determine risk exposure. Increase risk during strong trending periods when prices consistently trade in the direction of the trend and decrease exposure during range-bound or choppy market conditions.

3. News and Events:

- Monitor news and economic events alongside VWAP to adjust risk accordingly. Increase risk exposure during low-impact periods and reduce exposure during high-impact events to mitigate the impact of unexpected market movements.

Conclusion

Integrating VWAP analysis into risk management strategies enhances traders' ability to protect capital and optimize risk-reward ratios effectively. By setting stop-loss and take-profit levels with VWAP, adjusting position sizing based on VWAP deviations, and adapting risk based on market conditions, traders can manage risk more efficiently and navigate volatile market environments with confidence. VWAP provides traders with valuable insights into market dynamics and price trends, allowing for more informed risk management decisions and improved trading outcomes. In the subsequent chapters, we will explore practical applications and case studies of risk management strategies using VWAP analysis.

CHAPTER 25

TRADING ETFS WITH VWAP

Exchange-Traded Funds (ETFs) have become increasingly popular among traders and investors due to their ease of access, diversification benefits, and liquidity. VWAP (Volume Weighted Average Price) analysis can be a powerful tool for trading ETFs, allowing traders to navigate the unique market structure of ETFs, assess liquidity, and develop effective trading strategies. In this chapter, we will explore the market structure of ETFs, the role of liquidity in ETF trading, and how to create ETF trading strategies using VWAP analysis.

ETF Market Structure

1. Creation and Redemption:

- ETFs are investment funds that trade on stock exchanges, representing a basket of assets such as stocks, bonds, or commodities. Authorized Participants (APs) facilitate the creation and redemption of ETF shares by exchanging underlying assets with the ETF issuer.

2. Secondary Market Trading:

- ETF shares are traded on stock exchanges like individual stocks, allowing investors to buy and sell shares throughout the trading day. Market makers provide liquidity by quoting bid and ask prices, facilitating secondary market trading of ETF shares.

3. Arbitrage Mechanism:

- ETF prices are closely tied to the value of their underlying assets. APs engage in arbitrage activities to keep ETF prices in line with the net asset value (NAV) of the underlying assets by buying or selling ETF shares and underlying assets to profit from price discrepancies.

Liquidity and VWAP in ETFs

1. Liquidity Providers:

- Market makers and APs play a crucial role in providing liquidity to ETF markets by quoting bid and ask prices and facilitating order execution. ETF liquidity is influenced by factors such as trading volume, bid-ask spreads, and underlying asset liquidity.

2. VWAP Calculation:

- VWAP analysis in ETF trading considers both ETF trading volume and underlying asset volume. Traders assess VWAP deviations from the NAV to gauge market efficiency and liquidity conditions, adjusting trading strategies accordingly.

3. ETF Liquidity Profiles:

- Different ETFs may exhibit varying liquidity profiles based on factors such as asset class, market capitalization, and trading volume. Traders analyze VWAP dynamics and liquidity metrics to assess the liquidity risk of trading specific ETFs.

Creating ETF Trading Strategies with VWAP

1. Trend Confirmation:

- Use VWAP as a tool to confirm trend directions in ETFs and validate trading signals. Prices consistently trading above VWAP may indicate bullish trends, while prices below VWAP may suggest bearish trends, guiding trading decisions.

2. Rebalancing Strategies:

- Employ VWAP-based rebalancing strategies for ETF portfolios to optimize trade execution and minimize market impact. Execute buy or sell orders around VWAP to achieve efficient portfolio rebalancing while minimizing transaction costs.

3. Sector Rotation:

- Utilize VWAP analysis to implement sector rotation strategies using sector-specific ETFs. Monitor VWAP dynamics across different sectors to identify relative strength or weakness and allocate capital accordingly to sectors with favorable trends.

Conclusion

ETFs provide traders with diversified exposure to various asset classes and market sectors, making them attractive vehicles for implementing trading strategies. By incorporating VWAP analysis into ETF trading, traders can assess market structure, evaluate liquidity conditions, and develop effective trading strategies tailored to ETF markets. Understanding the market structure of ETFs, the role of liquidity in ETF trading, and how to create ETF trading strategies with VWAP analysis empowers traders to navigate ETF markets with confidence and achieve trading objectives effectively. In the subsequent chapters, we will explore practical applications and case studies of trading ETFs using VWAP analysis.

CHAPTER 26

VWAP AND MARKET

MANIPULATION

Market manipulation is a concern for traders and investors, as it can distort market prices, create artificial trading volumes, and undermine market integrity. VWAP (Volume Weighted Average Price) analysis can serve as a valuable tool for detecting market manipulation, protecting trades from manipulation, and reporting suspicious activities to relevant authorities. In this chapter, we will explore how VWAP can be used to identify signs of market manipulation, safeguard trades against manipulation, and take action against suspicious activities.

Detecting Market Manipulation with VWAP

1. Abnormal Price Movements:

- Monitor VWAP deviations and abnormal price movements that may indicate market manipulation. Sudden and significant deviations from VWAP without fundamental justification could signal manipulative activities aimed at influencing market prices.

2. Volume Spikes:

- Analyze volume spikes and unusual trading activity around VWAP to identify potential manipulation. Large volume trades executed near VWAP levels with no clear market rationale may suggest attempts to manipulate market prices.

3. VWAP Discrepancies:

- Compare VWAP calculations across different timeframes and trading venues to detect discrepancies that may indicate manipulation. Inconsistent VWAP values or significant deviations from expected VWAP levels could raise red flags for manipulation.

Protecting Your Trades from Manipulation

1. Diversify Trading Venues:

- Spread trading activity across multiple venues to reduce the risk of falling victim to manipulation on a single exchange. Diversifying trading venues allows traders to compare VWAP calculations and detect discrepancies more effectively.

2. Implement Risk Controls:

- Implement risk management controls, including stop-loss orders and position limits, to protect trades from manipulation-induced losses. Set predefined risk parameters based on VWAP deviations and abnormal market behavior to mitigate the impact of manipulation.

3. Stay Informed:

- Stay informed about market news, regulatory updates, and emerging trends in market manipulation tactics. Educate yourself on common manipulation techniques and remain vigilant for signs of suspicious activities that may affect your trades.

Reporting Suspicious Activities

1. Regulatory Authorities:

- Report suspicious activities to relevant regulatory authorities, such as the Securities and Exchange Commission (SEC) or the Financial Conduct Authority (FCA). Provide detailed information, including trade data, VWAP analysis, and any other evidence of market manipulation.

2. Trading Platforms:

- Report suspicious activities to trading platforms or exchanges where manipulative trades are detected. Work closely with platform administrators and compliance teams to investigate and address potential instances of market manipulation.

3. Industry Associations:

- Collaborate with industry associations and market participants to share information and raise awareness about market manipulation. Participate in industry forums, workshops, and initiatives aimed at combating market manipulation and promoting market integrity.

Conclusion

VWAP analysis can play a crucial role in detecting and combating market manipulation by providing traders with insights into market dynamics and abnormal trading patterns. By monitoring VWAP deviations, safeguarding trades against manipulation, and reporting suspicious activities to relevant authorities, traders can contribute to maintaining market integrity and protecting their interests. Understanding the signs of market manipulation, implementing risk controls, and taking proactive measures to report suspicious activities are essential for preserving market fairness and ensuring a level playing field for all market participants. In the subsequent chapters, we will explore practical applications and case studies of using VWAP analysis to detect and respond to market manipulation effectively.

CHAPTER 27

SOCIAL TRADING AND VWAP

Social trading platforms have revolutionized the way traders interact, share insights, and collaborate on investment strategies. By integrating VWAP (Volume Weighted Average Price) analysis into social trading, traders can leverage collective wisdom, copy trading strategies based on VWAP signals, and harness social media sentiment to inform their trading decisions. In this chapter, we will explore how social trading intersects with VWAP analysis, including copy trading with VWAP, incorporating social media sentiment into VWAP strategies, and community-based VWAP analysis.

Copy Trading with VWAP

1. Signal Providers:

- Follow experienced traders or signal providers who incorporate VWAP analysis into their trading strategies. Copy trades based on VWAP signals provided by signal providers, allowing you to replicate their trading decisions automatically.

2. VWAP-based Strategies:

- Choose signal providers who use VWAP as a primary indicator in their trading strategies. Look for providers who employ VWAP-based trend following, mean reversion, or breakout strategies that align with your trading objectives and risk tolerance.

3. Performance Monitoring:

- Monitor the performance of signal providers using VWAP-based strategies to assess their effectiveness over time. Evaluate key metrics such as win rate, average profit/loss, and drawdown to identify high-performing providers and optimize your copy trading portfolio.

Social Media Sentiment and VWAP

1. Sentiment Analysis:

- Monitor social media platforms for discussions, news, and sentiment related to financial markets and specific assets. Analyze sentiment indicators derived from social media data alongside VWAP analysis to gauge market sentiment and anticipate price movements.

2. VWAP Correlation:

- Identify correlations between social media sentiment and VWAP dynamics to validate trading signals and confirm market sentiment. Positive sentiment trends on social media platforms may align with bullish VWAP signals, while negative sentiment may coincide with bearish VWAP trends.

3. Event-driven Analysis:

- Monitor social media chatter and sentiment around significant market events, earnings releases, or economic announcements. Incorporate event-driven VWAP analysis to assess the impact of social media sentiment on market volatility and trading opportunities.

Community-Based VWAP Analysis

1. Collaborative Analysis:

- Participate in online trading communities or forums where traders share insights, strategies, and VWAP analysis. Collaborate with fellow traders to conduct VWAP analysis, validate trading ideas, and exchange feedback on market trends.

2. Crowd-sourced Strategies:

- Crowdsource trading strategies based on VWAP analysis within trading communities. Leverage the collective expertise and diverse perspectives of community members to develop robust VWAP-based strategies and adapt to changing market conditions.

3. Peer Review:

- Seek peer review and feedback on your VWAP analysis and trading strategies from other members of the trading community. Engage in constructive discussions, share trade ideas, and refine your VWAP-based strategies based on insights and suggestions from peers.

Conclusion

Social trading platforms offer traders unprecedented opportunities to collaborate, share insights, and harness collective wisdom in their trading endeavors. By integrating VWAP analysis into social trading, traders can leverage VWAP signals, incorporate social media sentiment, and engage in community-based analysis to enhance their trading decisions. Whether through copy trading with VWAP, monitoring social media sentiment, or collaborating with peers on VWAP analysis, social trading provides traders with valuable tools and resources to navigate financial markets effectively. In the subsequent chapters, we will explore practical applications and case studies of social trading strategies using VWAP analysis.

CHAPTER 28

CONTINUOUS LEARNING AND ADAPTATION

Continuous learning and adaptation are essential for traders to stay ahead in dynamic financial markets. By staying informed on market changes, evolving VWAP (Volume Weighted Average Price) strategies, and networking with other VWAP traders, traders can adapt to evolving market conditions, refine their trading approaches, and achieve long-term success. In this chapter, we will explore the importance of continuous learning and adaptation in VWAP trading and strategies for staying informed, evolving, and networking within the VWAP trading community.

Staying Informed on Market Changes

1. Market Research:

- Conduct regular market research to stay informed about macroeconomic trends, industry developments, and geopolitical events that may impact financial markets. Stay updated on news, reports, and market analysis from reputable sources to identify emerging opportunities and risks.

2. Economic Calendar:

- Monitor economic calendars for scheduled releases of key economic indicators, central bank announcements, and geopolitical events. Anticipate market volatility and plan trading strategies around high-impact events to capitalize on potential price movements.

3. Market Analysis Tools:

- Utilize market analysis tools, such as charting platforms, news aggregators, and market scanners, to analyze market trends, identify trading opportunities, and assess market sentiment. Incorporate VWAP analysis alongside other technical indicators to make informed trading decisions.

Evolving Your VWAP Strategies

1. Strategy Evaluation:

- Regularly evaluate the performance of your VWAP strategies using historical data, backtesting, and performance metrics. Identify strengths, weaknesses, and areas for improvement to refine and optimize your trading approaches over time.

2. Adaptation to Market Conditions:

- Adapt VWAP strategies to changing market conditions, volatility levels, and trading environments. Modify VWAP parameters, timeframes, or trading rules to align with prevailing market trends and optimize trade execution efficiency.

3. Innovation and Experimentation:

- Embrace innovation and experimentation in VWAP trading by exploring new ideas, techniques, and trading methodologies. Test alternative VWAP strategies, incorporate emerging technologies, and adapt to evolving market dynamics to stay ahead of the curve.

Networking with Other VWAP Traders

1. Online Communities:

- Join online forums, social media groups, and trading communities focused on VWAP analysis and trading. Engage with fellow VWAP traders, share insights, and exchange ideas on VWAP strategies, market trends, and trading best practices.

2. Webinars and Workshops:

- Attend webinars, workshops, and seminars conducted by VWAP experts, trading professionals, and industry leaders. Learn from experienced traders, gain valuable insights into VWAP analysis techniques, and stay updated on the latest trends in VWAP trading.

3. Mentorship and Collaboration:

- Seek mentorship and collaboration opportunities with experienced VWAP traders who can provide guidance, feedback, and support in your trading journey. Learn from their experiences, leverage their expertise, and collaborate on VWAP analysis projects to accelerate your learning and development.

Conclusion

Continuous learning and adaptation are integral to success in VWAP trading and financial markets. By staying informed on market changes, evolving VWAP strategies, and networking with other VWAP traders, traders can enhance their knowledge, skills, and trading performance over time. Embrace a growth mindset, remain open to new ideas, and actively engage in the VWAP trading community to stay ahead of the competition and achieve long-term success in your trading endeavors. In the subsequent chapters, we will explore practical applications and case studies of continuous learning and adaptation in VWAP trading.

CHAPTER 29

THE FUTURE OF VWAP TRADING

As financial markets continue to evolve, so too does the practice of VWAP (Volume Weighted Average Price) trading. Traders must stay ahead of emerging trends, leverage technological advancements, and adapt to future developments to remain competitive and profitable. In this chapter, we will explore the future of VWAP trading, including emerging trends, technological advancements, and strategies for incorporating future developments into your trading approach.

Emerging Trends in VWAP Trading

1. AI and Machine Learning:

- The integration of artificial intelligence (AI) and machine learning (ML) into VWAP trading algorithms is expected to increase. Advanced algorithms can analyze vast amounts of data, identify complex patterns, and optimize trade execution strategies with greater precision.

2. Quantitative Analysis:

- Quantitative analysis techniques, such as algorithmic trading and high-frequency trading (HFT), will continue to play a significant role in VWAP trading. Traders will rely on quantitative models to automate trading decisions and exploit short-term market inefficiencies.

3. ESG Investing:

- Environmental, social, and governance (ESG) factors are becoming increasingly important for investors. Traders may incorporate ESG criteria into VWAP trading strategies, aligning investments with sustainability goals and societal values.

Technological Advancements in VWAP Analysis

1. Big Data Analytics:

- The use of big data analytics tools will enable traders to analyze large datasets and extract actionable insights for VWAP trading. Advanced analytics techniques can uncover hidden patterns, correlations, and market trends to inform trading decisions.

2. High-Frequency Trading Platforms:

- High-frequency trading (HFT) platforms will continue to evolve, offering ultra-fast execution speeds and low-latency connectivity. Traders will leverage HFT platforms to execute VWAP strategies with minimal delay and capitalize on fleeting market opportunities.

3. Blockchain Technology:

- Blockchain technology has the potential to revolutionize financial markets by providing transparent, decentralized trading platforms. Traders may explore blockchain-based VWAP trading platforms, offering enhanced security, transparency, and efficiency.

Incorporating Future Developments into Your Trading Strategies

1. Adaptive Strategies:

- Develop adaptive VWAP trading strategies that can adjust to evolving market conditions, technological advancements, and regulatory changes. Incorporate flexibility into your trading approach to capitalize on emerging trends and opportunities.

2. Continuous Learning:

- Stay informed about the latest developments in VWAP trading, technology, and market trends. Continuously educate yourself through research, training, and networking to remain at the forefront of VWAP trading innovation.

3. Risk Management:

- Prioritize risk management in your VWAP trading strategies, especially in the face of technological advancements and market uncertainties. Implement robust risk controls, diversify your portfolio, and monitor risk exposure to protect capital and preserve profitability.

Conclusion

The future of VWAP trading holds immense potential for innovation, growth, and opportunity. By embracing emerging trends, leveraging technological advancements, and adapting to future developments, traders can position themselves for success in dynamic financial markets. Stay proactive, flexible, and informed to navigate the evolving landscape of VWAP trading effectively. Incorporate adaptive strategies, prioritize continuous learning, and emphasize risk management to thrive in the future of VWAP trading. In the subsequent chapters, we will explore practical applications and case studies of future-oriented VWAP trading strategies.